Everything You Need To Know About

EATING DISORDERS

ANOREXIA AND BULIMIA

An eating disorder can make any meal an uncomfortable experience.

• THE NEED TO KNOW LIBRARY •

Everything You Need To Know About

EATING DISORDERS

ANOREXIA AND BULIMIA

Rachel Kubersky, M.P.H.

THE ROSEN PUBLISHING GROUP, INC.
NEW YORK

Published in 1992 by The Rosen Publishing Group, Inc.
29 East 21st Street, New York, NY 10010

First Edition
Copyright 1992 by The Rosen Publishing Group, Inc.

Printed in the United States of America

Library of Congress Cataloging-in-Publication Data

Kubersky, Rachel.
    Everything you need to know about eating disorders / Rachel
Kubersky.
        (The Need to know library)
        Includes bibliographical references and index.
        Summary: Discusses eating disorders, the role of food in our
lives, and how to stay healthy physically and mentally.
        ISBN 0-8239-1321-X
        1. Anorexia nervosa—Juvenile literature. 2. Bulimia—Juvenile
literature. [1. Anorexia nervosa. 2. Bulimia. 3. Eating disorders.
4. Food—Psychological aspects.] I. Title. II. Series.
RC552.A5K83   1992
616.85'26—dc20   91-46600
                                                              CIP
                                                              AC

Contents

Introduction

Young people are especially at risk for the development of eating disorders. An eating disorder is a puzzling and complex health problem. The visible signs of this disease show up only after you have become very ill. The problem begins long before any physical damage has been done.

The cause of eating disorders is not yet fully understood. Each disorder starts in the mind. If you have an eating disorder you may see and feel things differently from what they really are. But like the diseases that are caused by viruses and bacteria, eating disorders must be treated as soon as possible. If not treated they can cause serious illness and death. One out of ten people die from their eating disorder.

People as young as 10 can suffer from eating disorders. Most people who have eating disorders are between the ages of 14 and 20. Nine out of ten are female.

Over the past 30 years the number of people with eating disorders has grown. Some experts believe that there is an epidemic. It is estimated that over a million Americans develop *anorexia nervosa* and *bulimia* each year. Those are the two most common disorders. Eating disorders are an especially big problem on college campuses.

For years little was known about anorexia nervosa and bulimia. Anorexia nervosa is sometimes called the "starving disease." But bulimia involves first grossly overeating, then getting rid of the food in an unhealthy way.

As the number of people having these disorders has grown, more people have come to know someone who has one of them.

A number of celebrities have suffered from eating disorders. Karen Carpenter, a well-known pop singer, was one of these celebrities. She died from heart failure, a common result of anorexia nervosa. Her death brought the discussion of eating disorders out in the open. There was talk about it on television and radio. Books were written on the subject. Stories based on real-life people with eating disorders appeared on television.

Information about the seriousness of eating disorders has been spreading. The resulting knowledge has enabled people with disorders to get help. It has saved lives.

For many teens, rituals surrounding food are an important part of being social.

Chapter 1

Food in Our Lives

"A man cannot be too serious about his eating, for food is the force that binds society together."

–Confucius

Food is part of our everyday lives. You need food to stay alive. Food, or the lack of it, influences how you feel. When you are hungry you may feel tired or cranky. If your hunger is not satisfied you may even get a headache or feel dizzy. A body that has not had food for a long time no longer works very well. It is not able to do ordinary chores well. And it cannot think clearly.

Food for you, as for any other living thing, is most important.

Food and Feelings

Food may also influence your emotions. Most of us associate certain foods with certain feelings. For example, some foods may give you the good feeling of being cared for. For some people that food might be chicken soup. For others it might be mashed potatoes or macaroni and cheese. Someone else may associate this feeling of safety and well-being with chocolate ice cream or cooked greens.

Foods that make you feel cared for are often called "comfort foods." Your feelings about foods usually develop at an early age.

It is easy to understand why we often associate food with comfort. Your earliest experience with food involved being held, cared for, and fed. Whether you were fed from a bottle or from your mother's breast, you were held close. The good feeling of being held was linked to being fed.

Your need to be fed also made your parents listen to you. When you cried, you told those taking care of you that you were hungry. Then you were not only fed, but also held close.

Food and Traditions

Food and drink, from the earliest times, have played an important part in all sorts of celebrations. Certain sweet spices are used in the baking of Christmas cookies, for example. They are symbols of the gifts of spices that the Wise Men brought to the Infant Jesus.

During the holiday of Hanukkah, people eat potato pancakes fried in oil. The pancakes are fried in oil to celebrate the miracle of one day's supply of oil burning for eight days.

Blackeyed peas, thought to bring good luck in Africa, are still served for that reason in the area of the Caribbean and in the southern United States on New Year's Eve. And what would Thanksgiving be without turkey and cranberry sauce?

The sharing of food, eating with others, makes people feel closer to each other. Many people who live alone say that food tastes much better when eaten in company.

People associate certain foods with certain activities. You are probably familiar with the sound and smell of popcorn in the movie theater. Hot dogs and roasted peanuts may remind you of base-ball games.

Your family may have its own food traditions. One year Joe's grandmother prepared a special chocolate dessert for a family gathering. Every-body loved it. From that day on whenever Joe's family got together, his grandmother made that dish. After Joe's grandmother died his uncle Paul took over making it. That particular dish, its taste and smell, became associated with family get-togethers and good times for Joe's whole family.

Likes and Dislikes

Each of us has our own personal associations with food. You probably like some foods more than others. You may even say that you "love" a particular food. That may be simply because you have good memories associated with it. Maggie, who is now a grown woman, remembers the wonderful mashed potatoes her mother fed her when she was ill as a little girl. That food made her feel loved. To this day, whenever Maggie feels sick, she fixes herself fluffy mashed potatoes.

On the other hand you may strongly dislike some foods because you have unpleasant memories of them. Michael is 16 years old. He is not a fussy eater. He will eat almost anything except for bananas and cooked cereal. Michael hates these foods so much that he finds it difficult just to look at them. Michael also knows why he dislikes these foods. He was forced to eat them as a child. Many of us who have similar problems with certain foods often do not know why.

Meredith, 15, looked forward each year to Thanksgiving. It was one of her favorite days. It included her favorite foods. It was always happy and relaxed. The house smelled so good from all that wonderful cooking. Meredith loved her mother's roast turkey with all the fixings. She particularly liked the sweet potato pie.

One year, shortly before Thanksgiving, Meredith decided to work as a volunteer in a local nursing home. She felt good about contributing her time this way. She looked forward to the new experience, even though she was anxious about it. There were sights, sounds, and smells in the home that she would have to get used to. Some of them were not pleasant.

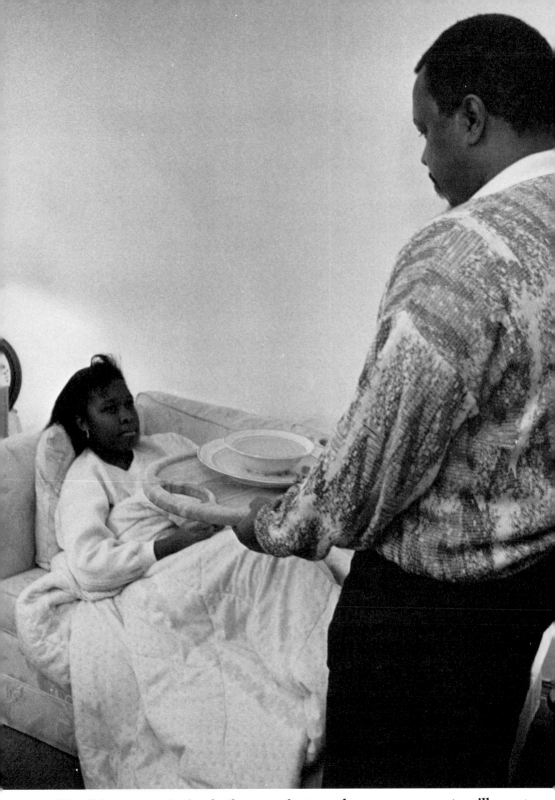

We all have certain foods that comfort us when we are upset or ill.

On Thanksgiving day she helped serve dinner to the residents at the nursing home. It was a very special meal that included all of Meredith's favorite Thanksgiving foods—even sweet potato pie. But in this setting they no longer appealed to her. In fact, she felt queasy and couldn't eat any of the meal. Her feelings about being with old and sick people made Meredith uncomfortable. She associated her discomfort with the various odors of the nursing home, and with the food smells. The experience changed her feelings for some of her favorite foods.

What you eat also depends on how you feel. Some of us may stop eating when we feel nervous, scared, depressed, or lonely. We may even feel sick to the stomach when we experience these feelings. For others, these same feelings may bring on a need to overeat. If that happens once in a while it is okay. But when someone allows overeating or undereating to become a routine way of expressing feelings, that person may become unhealthy.

Eating can give you pleasure. We often share this enjoyment with friends and family. Eating also nourishes your body.

Fasting means not eating or drinking for a period of time. Some people fast for religious reasons. Some people fast for health reasons. They believe that it is good to give the body a rest from eating and digesting. But other people fast too much. We will talk about different kinds of unhealthy fasting.

Chapter 2

The Pressure to Be Thin

We are fortunate to live in a time and place where we have lots of choices of what to eat. There is also plenty of food available.

Not only do we enjoy a great variety of foods, but many of these foods have already been prepared for us. One type of prepared food is called fast food. Fast food is advertised on the radio and TV, in newspapers and magazines, and on billboards. So even if you are not hungry or thirsty you are often reminded of food.

The Weight-Control Craze

At the same time, however, you are reminded to be thin and to control your appetite. You are told that being overweight is bad for your health. You are told that extra fat is unattractive.

We admire people for being thin. We comment on people's weight when we greet them. It is meant to be a compliment when we say, "Hey, you lost weight." On the other hand, someone may say to us, "Hey, you put on a little weight." Usually that is not something we like to hear.

Mary Lou, 16, was an honor student. She had a lovely voice and sang in the school chorus, often as a soloist. She wrote for the school newspaper. Some of her stories had won prizes in national competitions. She was an attractive, happy girl with lots of friends. One summer Mary Lou decided that she needed to improve her figure. When she looked at all the very thin models in the magazines, she felt fat. So she decided to lose weight.

Mary Lou went on several reducing diets that her friends had recommended. Her parents disapproved of her dieting. They noticed that she had become cranky and moody. She was not acting like herself. But they could not persuade her to stop dieting.

After two months she had lost fifteen pounds. She looked thinner. Her hips, though, were still not as slim as she wanted them to be. Everyone noticed the weight loss and complimented her on it. A fuss was made over her simply because she was thinner. But she didn't really feel better about herself. On the contrary, feeling hungry all the time made her feel deprived and miserable.

A distorted body image is nearly always a part of any eating disorder.

Magazines and newspapers are filled with images of thin people who are supposed to be the ideal of beauty for all.

Fortunately for Mary Lou, she realized that something was wrong. She thought it was odd that she was getting more praise for her weight loss than she had ever gotten for her other achievements. She talked to her parents about her feelings. Finally she decided to go back to eating the way she always had. It was a relief to eat what everyone else in the family was eating. Now she didn't have to think constantly about what she was going to eat.

Mary Lou was able to get on with her life. She had time and energy for her writing, her music, her schoolwork, and her friends. She felt good again. She decided that even though her figure was not like the models' in the swimsuit ads, it suited her just fine.

Where did Mary Lou get the idea that she needed to be thinner? For one thing, everyone around her talked about being thin and dieting. Classmates who were overweight were talked about, almost as if they had committed a crime. Wherever Mary Lou looked, it seemed to her, she was faced by perfect bodies. Television, magazines, and, of course, the movies all showed off these perfect figures. It was harder to find them in real life. But there they were on the screen and in the magazines, usually selling something to do with weight control.

You too probably hear about formerly over-weight people who are now thin. They say that losing all that weight was the best thing that ever happened to them. They swear that they will never be fat again. But most do regain the weight.

How often have we heard people comment, "She would be so pretty if only she'd lose a few pounds," or, "He would be so handsome if only he were not so heavy."

A lot of our ideas about weight come from watching TV and reading magazines. We see dozens of ads for foods promising to make us slim. Health clubs urge us to shape up and get rid of our fat. The advertisements always show tall, thin, and attractive models.

Do you ever go through a day without hearing or seeing something about weight control? Keep a record, one day, of all the messages that you see and hear about being slim, losing weight, and dieting. Count the times, too, when your family, your friends, your parents' friends, or anyone else you know talks about losing weight.

We spend over $10 billion a year in efforts to lose weight. We buy diet books. We buy special foods and food supplements. We buy exercise machines. We buy special clothing to help us sweat off pounds as we exercise. We spend all this money in the hope of becoming slim. Most of us don't want to be thin to be healthier. We want to be slim to be more attractive.

Changing Ideas of "Fat" and "Thin"

Where do we get our ideas as to how fat or thin we should be? For the past 25 years it has been fashionable to be thin. Models who wear the latest fashions in magazines have been very thin. "The thinner the better" is how most people have tended to think about weight.

But our ideas about fatness and thinness have changed over the years. That is especially true of women's figures. Long ago, for example, it was fashionable for women to have big hips and big

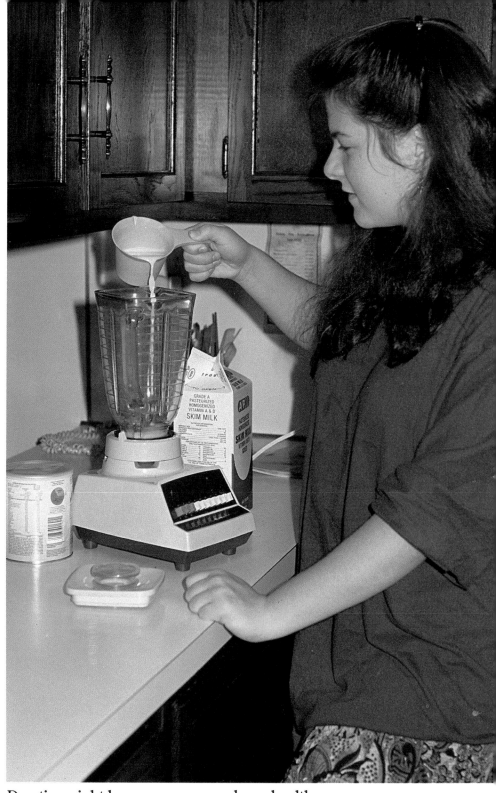

Drastic weight loss programs can be unhealthy—even dangerous—for a person with an eating disorder.

breasts. Clothes were designed to show off the hips and breasts.

The words we use to describe body size tend to change, depending on how we think about fatness and thinness. When bigger was more fashionable, we used words like full-figured, plump, and cuddly to describe certain people. Today, those people would probably be called fat.

At one time being heavy was a status symbol. It was hard for many people to get enough to eat each day. If you were fat it meant that you were well off. Thinness was associated with being poor. And because the poor were often sick, being thin was also thought to be unhealthy.

More recently, however, thinness has become desirable. We use words like *slim* and *trim* for a look that in the past would have been described as skeletal and unattractive.

We are influenced by what our culture decides is fat or thin. For some of us that is a big problem. We can't fit into a mold someone else has chosen for us.

The Importance of Healthful Eating

In our drive to become thin, many of us do not eat healthfully. Each of us has a different body type and different food needs. Some people are very active. Some people spend a lot of time sitting down. Some of us are old, some very young. We have different needs at different times in our lives.

A woman who is pregnant needs to eat more than a woman who is not. Athletes who expend a lot of energy have to make sure they eat enough healthful food. When we are recuperating from illness our bodies may require more nourishment to be able to recover completely.

Not eating properly can create health problems. This is especially true of young people. Active young people need well-nourished bodies. Young bodies cannot grow on diet sodas that contain only one calorie.

Plain vegetables and diet soda do not make a healthy, well-rounded meal for a growing teen.

Restricting calories may make you thin, but it will not always be good for you. Dieting too much is more harmful to young bodies than being a little overweight.

Your job as a responsible person is to learn as much about eating healthfully as you can. There are so many things you can eat that are delicious and are good for you. You and your body need to be fed properly.

How Do You Think about Food?

1. When you haven't eaten in a long time, how do you feel physically? Do you feel tired, weak, or even faint?
2. If you are very hungry, how do you feel emotionally? Can you describe those feelings?
3. What food or foods, if any, give you a feeling of being cared for? Do you know why?
4. What are some of your favorite foods associated with family, religious, or national holidays and celebrations?
5. What food or foods, if any, do you strongly dislike? Do you remember when you first developed this dislike?
6. Do you ever eat because you are bored or feeling lonely?
7. Do you know what activities make you want to eat, whether or not you are hungry?
8. Can you name any foods with smells that you associate with certain feelings?
9. Do you ever use food to reward yourself?

Chapter 3

What Are Eating Disorders?

Eating disorders have been around for a long time. The two we discuss in this book are anorexia nervosa (sometimes called just anorexia) and bulimia. People suffering from anorexia are called anorectics. People suffering from bulimia are called bulimics.

When Do Eating Disorders Happen?

Eating disorders occur when you use eating, or not eating, to try to control your life. They also involve expressing your feelings through the use of food. If you have trouble accepting yourself as you are, you may believe that your life would be perfect if only you could be thin. Then you may put all your energy into becoming and staying thin.

25

But life cannot be perfect. So if you are counting on thinness to make your life perfect, you will never feel thin enough. And you will never feel you have lost enough weight.

Anorectics do not see themselves as they really are. They never see themselves as thin, even when to others they look like living skeletons. That is part of the problem. They have a distorted image of themselves.

Historical Views of Eating Disorders

A form of what we now call anorexia was seen in the Middle Ages, over 500 years ago. Then it was called *anorexia mirabilis.* The term means a loss of appetite caused by a miracle. In those days many women refused to eat. Their fasting was considered miraculous, and they were considered very special people.

Some religious young women fasted to repent for their sins. They were admired for their ability to live on the smallest amount of food. One of these women was made a saint. She was called Saint Catherine of Siena. She ate no more than a spoonful of herbs a day. Not eating became a symbol for being especially holy and devout.

Two hundred years later that kind of fasting was no longer considered miraculous and it came to be discouraged by the Church. It was thought to be inspired by the devil. So a great effort was made to stop such behavior.

Saint Catherine of Siena expressed her religious devotion by fasting for long periods of time.

In the late 19th century, fasting and starving were looked upon in yet a different way. Science and medicine had made advances. Doctors and scientists were able to identify and name diseases. But they were not yet able to cure them.

Loss of appetite was considered a symptom of many diseases. People were thought to lose their appetite as a result of cancer, stomach diseases, and the nausea of early pregnancy. But few people believed that loss of appetite, or the refusal to eat, could actually be a disease itself.

Doctors found it hard to believe that people would deliberately starve themselves. They felt certain that a separate disease was causing this "lack of appetite." So they kept looking for physical reasons.

Sir William Withey Gull was a well-known English doctor. Around 1870, he came to the conclusion that there was a "starving disease" that began in the patient's mind. He is believed to have been the first person to call the disease anorexia nervosa. The word *nervosa* refers to the mind.

At the same time doctors in France and the United States saw and described similar cases. They came to the same conclusions as Dr. Gull.

Possible Causes

Exactly what causes the mind to "misthink" in this way is still not completely known. There may be many reasons.

Even though anorectics refuse to eat, they will often take charge of meals for other people.

Some doctors believe that one cause may be not wanting to face adulthood. By keeping his or her body thin, preventing it from growing properly, the anorectic (and bulimic) may be expressing a fear of growing up.

Another theory is that people with eating disorders want to be special. They see everyone around them struggling with their appetite. They believe that by living on practically no food they can prove themselves to be special and unique. They can feel superhuman, or "above it all."

Control over others may be still another reason. Those ill with these disorders can upset parents, friends, and teachers by not eating. As they become thinner everyone around them becomes concerned.

Even though they refuse to eat, anorectics often take charge of family meals. They may bake and cook for family, friends, and classmates. In this way, they can control what they do not eat and what others do eat.

Some experts believe there is a link between eating disorders and child abuse. Victims of abuse often feel they have no control over their lives. Eating, or not eating, becomes very important to these victims. They *can* control their diet. It may be the only way they believe they can take charge of what happens to them.

Adolescence is also a difficult time to establish a positive self-image. Both boys and girls go through dramatic physical changes in a short time. When you are a teen, every time you look in the mirror you may see a change. You may experience a lot of ups and downs, or mood swings.

Peter was struggling to gain a good self-image. He was 15, and he wanted to be noticed. He was very bright and a good student. He was competitive in everything he did. He also tended to be critical of both friends and family. Peter was popular in school but did not have any really close friends. In that sense he was a loner.

Peter was used to getting his way at home. His parents, both busy professionals, didn't spend much time with him. They were intimidated by his constant criticism of them. They usually gave in to his demands. He was good at playing one parent against the other, but he wasn't really happy with that. He wished his parents would stand up to him. But he thought they didn't care enough for him to do so.

Peter's parents were extremely generous in buying him things and giving him money. He only had to mention that he wanted something, and there it was.

Peter took up tennis so he could play with his father and was very competitive when they played. There was never a happy ending to their games. If Peter didn't win he was totally depressed. When he did win, he thought his father hadn't tried his best. And then Peter would sulk.

Eating disorders may turn the family dinner table into a battleground.

Peter also took up running. He wanted to become really fit and thin. He wanted to become the best runner around. He read up on running and dieting. He followed a very rigorous training schedule. He had a long list of foods he thought were bad for him, and he continued to cut down on his portions of food. Family mealtimes usually ended in a big argument.

Peter lost weight, but he still did not like the way he looked. He ate even less. He increased his running time and mileage. But even that didn't seem enough. His dieting and his running took control of him. No matter how much weight he lost and no matter how much he ran, it was never enough.

At the end of eight months Peter's weight had dropped from 135 pounds to 95 pounds. He looked like a skeleton.

His parents were very upset and insisted that he see a doctor. There were many arguments. Peter insisted that he felt just fine. But he reluctantly kept the doctor's appointment his parents made for him. He continued his argument with the doctor. He insisted that his weight was at last becoming just right for running.

Peter's condition had become so serious that he could not be treated at home. He had to be put in the hospital until he had gained some weight back. He was seriously ill from the effects of starvation. After years of getting help with his problems, Peter finally recovered.

Dieting becomes dangerous when it rules every minute of your day.

Chapter 4

Anorexia: When Dieting Goes Too Far

J ust when you are most confused by all the changes happening in you as you become an adult, you pick up messages from TV, radio, and magazine ads telling you how you ought to look. The ads are for beautiful skin, thin bodies, silky hair, and long, manicured nails. It is not possible to look like the models in the ads all the time, if ever.

Images from ads probably help bring on eating disorders. But whatever the cause, if you have any eating disorder, you should get help as quickly as possible. That is why it is important to know the symptoms of eating disorders.

The Dieting Fad
You probably know someone on a diet. It may even be you. The word diet is used to refer to what

someone ate on a regular basis. If you were asked what your diet was like, you were simply being asked what you ate day after day. Today the word usually refers to eating in a special way in order to lose weight.

Dieting has become very fashionable. Many people believe that it is something they ought to do. Dieting is often a topic of conversation.

We have been told so often that thin is good, healthy, and beautiful. But how thin is good? And should everyone be thin?

Fear of being fat makes people, particularly girls and women, limit what they eat. Dieting for weight loss is a serious business. It should never be done without the guidance of a health professional. This is especially true for teenagers. Teens often go on diets to become thin. But the teen years may not be the best time in one's life to diet for the sake of looking thin.

Not eating properly can be bad for your health, especially if you are growing. The food you eat should be carefully chosen. Each meal should be as nourishing as possible. Watching what you eat is important not only for weight loss. It is important because you need to eat well for your body to grow and develop healthily.

It is not easy to be casual about dieting. If you are dieting you may worry about whether you will succeed. You may worry about whether you will look as well as you had hoped after those pounds

Bulimics "binge" by eating a lot of food and then "purge" by causing themselves to vomit.

The Dangers of Bulimia

Bulimic behavior is as dangerous to your health as anorexic starving. Bulimics are less likely to die than are anorectics, but some bulimics have choked to death on their own vomit.

Constant vomiting can cause serious damage. Large amounts of strong acid are brought up from the stomach. In the stomach, this acid aids the digestion of food. But in the mouth, this acid destroys the enamel of the teeth and causes them to rot. The gums are also affected.

Repeated vomiting can also injure the *esophagus*. The esophagus is a muscular tube about nine inches long that carries food from the mouth to the stomach. Repeated vomiting can cause the walls of this tube to tear and bleed. If the bleeding cannot be stopped promptly, it can cause death.

Using a combination of laxatives and water pills can also be fatal. A mineral imbalance occurs from the loss of so much fluid from the body. This can affect the heart rhythm.

Emily, 14, had become self-conscious about her figure. Some of her friends told her she was getting chubby. The truth was that her body was changing. Her figure was becoming fuller. This was normal for her age.

Emily's parents had a lot of fashionable friends. Emily knew how important it was to them to remain slim. She heard her parents and their friends speak unkindly about people who were fat.

Emily became afraid of getting fat. She started to diet to lose weight. But feeling hungry all the time made her miserable. Her parents traveled a lot, and she was often home alone.

One day a friend told Emily that she had found the answer to the problem of becoming fat. She told Emily how to make herself vomit and how to use laxatives and water pills. Emily was thrilled the first time she tried vomiting. The huge amount of food she had eaten was all there in the toilet bowl—instead of adding pounds to her body. She really believed that this was the greatest possible solution to the problem of becoming fat.

Sometimes it was hard to hide what she was doing. And she did feel ashamed. She also hated lying to her parents. She made up excuses to explain why she always ran from the table right after dinner.

Emily bought the laxatives and the water pills. She also began using diet pills. Some days she did nothing but purge herself. She had become addicted to the behavior. She would need a lot of help and time to recover.

Emily believed she had found the way to have a thin body through bulimic behavior. Many of us follow unhealthy patterns of eating and dieting. When we eat too much of something, we may feel guilty. We may not eat the next day. Or we may exercise too much. Many people fast for a few days when a big party is coming up. That's so they feel they can eat a lot.

Mary, 20, is tall and very attractive. She is not really thin or fat. Her bones are broad and her hips are wide. That is how Mary's body is made. Everyone in her family is built that way. Mary is engaged to be married. She wants to look really slim on her wedding day. So Mary decided that before buying her wedding gown she would diet and become at least one size smaller. She wanted her hips, in particular, to become smaller.

It was very hard for Mary to lose the weight. She was upset that the pounds didn't come off quickly. She was hungry all the time. And she was miserable. One day, Mary couldn't stand her hunger pains any longer. She stuffed herself with all the goodies she had given up. That night she felt so sick that she actually threw up. Mary thought she had found the answer to her weight problem—purging! To her, being thin for her wedding was worth any price. She had to look "just right."

Mary wanted to look like the models in the bridal magazines. What she didn't realize was that we can't "copy" how others look. We are all different. We each have our own style. And we each have our own unique "look."

Chapter 6

Keeping Your Body Healthy

How do you avoid getting an eating disorder? Unfortunately, there is no *one* thing you can do that will prevent you from getting anorexia nervosa or bulimia. No vaccination or pills can keep you from getting an eating disorder.

Avoiding eating disorders takes a lot of work and awareness; the same things you would do to prevent most illnesses. You have to work at keeping yourself as healthy as you can—not only physically, but mentally healthy too.

Taking Care of Yourself

You have been given this wonderful human being—you—to take care of. This is a job for the rest of your life.

Let's look at how you can take care of your physical health. What does your body need?

You probably learned many ways to avoid getting hurt as you grew up. These reminders may sound familiar:

• Look both ways when crossing the street; cross only when the light is green.

• Buckle up when riding in a car.

• Wear a helmet when skateboarding, bike riding, or motorcycle riding.

• Wear warm clothes in winter.

• Use an effective sunscreen to prevent a summer sunburn.

Another important thing you can do for your health is to have regular medical and dental check-ups. That may help to catch small problems before they become bigger problems. It is always a good idea to ask questions when you visit the doctor and the dentist. Be sure to talk about anything that is bothering you.

Exercise

Exercise is important. It will keep you fit and relaxed. Being physically active can help you let off steam and keep you feeling good. It doesn't matter what you do. It can be playing ball, dancing, running, or doing gymnastics. But it should be something you enjoy.

Always exercise in *moderation*. That means do it sensibly. Don't overdo it. You are in charge. Find out how much exercise is comfortable for you. Know your own limits.

While daily exercise is good, overexercising can cause serious problems of exhaustion, injury, and malnutrition.

Eating Healthily

Another way we can try to stay healthy is to eat sensibly. What is sensible eating? Here again it is a good idea to follow the road of moderation. Moderation simply means avoiding extremes. It means staying within reasonable limits. Too much of anything is not good for you.

Betty had to learn about moderation the hard way. She thought that drinking lots of water was a good thing. It is. Water is good for you. She had read an article that described how drinking water flushed and cleansed your body. It was supposed to be particularly good for your skin.

Like most boys and girls her age, Betty thought she had a problem with her skin. At 16, Betty cared a lot about how she looked. So she started drinking water. She drank so much water that she had no room in her stomach for anything else. Drinking all that water was causing problems she had never expected.

Try not to label foods as "fat" or "thin" foods. Don't label foods as either "bad" or "good." It is the way we use foods that makes them good or bad for us. There is one exception, however. If you are allergic to a certain food, any amount of that food is bad for you. It could even be deadly. But that is not the case with most foods.

Vary what you eat. We have so many choices of foods. Become an explorer. Promise yourself that you will try any new food that is offered to you. If you don't like it, don't ask for more. But if you have not tried it, you will never know whether you like it or not. If you don't like a certain food at first, try it again some other time. Your tastes will change as you get older.

Most food experts today agree that you should eat few fatty foods and lots of fresh fruits and vegetables. You should also eat plenty of grains. Rice and wheat are good examples of grains. And you should avoid too much candy and cake. Try to satisfy your sweet tooth with natural sweets, like fruits and juices.

Snack foods sometimes cause problems. We usually eat them when we are hungry, maybe because we skipped a meal. Often we eat snack foods when we are in a hurry.

When we think of snack foods, most of us think of the commercial snacks that come in individual packages. Most of these snacks are actually prepared to tease your taste buds into eating more than you need. They are very sweet or very salty, sometimes both. They often contain a lot of fat. Our taste buds like salty, sweet, and fatty foods. That is why it is hard to stop eating them.

Snacking itself is not bad. There are times when you need something between meals. But you can save money and have snacks that are good for you if you avoid packaged snacks. If you have an allowance that you now regularly spend on snack foods, try saving it. Create your snacks with healthier, less expensive foods. Try nuts, fresh fruit, cheese, dried fruit, popcorn, or just plain crackers. Cut up celery sticks, carrot sticks, or any other vegetable you like and snack on that. You know what time of day you usually get hungry. Plan ahead and carry your snack with you.

Think before you eat. That way you will make better choices.

The *way* you eat is also important. Set aside time for relaxed, unhurried eating. Eating slowly will help you to digest your food more easily. It also gives you a chance to make your meals special. Relaxed meals can be a time to look forward to.

Daily family meals—that is, meals eaten at a certain time with most or all family members—have become a thing of the past. Today, family meals generally occur only on special occasions. Some experts believe that this may have encouraged the rise in eating disorders. Do your part in your family to have more meals together. Try to arrange for at least one or two others to eat with you. Let your family know that being together for meals is important to you.

Chapter 7

Keeping Your Mind Healthy

You are more than just a body with different parts that have to be looked after. What makes us humans special is that all our parts are affected by everything that goes on in our bodies and in our minds. You not only have to learn to take care of your body, but also to become aware of what is happening in your mind. To avoid eating disorders, you need to stay healthy mentally.

Who Are You?

Get to know yourself. That may sound silly at first. "Of course I know myself," you may say. "After all, I am me."

But you may be surprised at how much you can learn about yourself. It can be an adventure. Try to look at yourself as others might look at you. Try the following exercise. First describe yourself.

Begin by describing your body. What does it look like? Try not to judge yourself. You might even want to draw a picture of yourself.

Next, describe what you are like on the inside. Can you talk about your feelings? Do you know what makes you happy? Do you know what makes you sad? Do you know what you are afraid of? Do you know what you like or dislike?

Then make two lists. Label one, "Things I Like about Myself." Label the other, "Things I Do Not Like about Myself."

On the "Things I Do Not Like" list put an *x* next to the things *you* most want to change. Is your list fair and realistic? Did you put an *x* where you thought *someone else* might want you to change?

You may want to share your list with a friend and have him or her do the same exercise. You may be surprised to see how different you seem to someone else, even to someone who knows you well.

Emphasize the Positive

Many of us are too critical of ourselves. A little self-criticism is all right. It makes us want to change some things about ourselves. But we should not forget all the good things about ourselves.

Remind yourself that you have many good qualities. Give yourself frequent pats on the back. Think about your strengths. Think often about all the things that you do well. Then it will be easier to remember your good qualities when you feel down.

Having a group of close friends can help to ease the emotional pain of dealing with an eating disorder.

Keep in mind that no one is perfect. There is no such thing as a perfect life or a perfect person. But that does not mean that we should just give up and never try to do better or be better. You have chances to try to improve yourself every day. Use these chances to grow as a person.

Growth is often painful. Change is hard. It is hard to deal with unfamiliar feelings and situations. But these things are also part of the challenge and adventure of life.

Accept yourself as you are. Be kind to yourself. Be aware of what you can change. Also be clear about those things over which you have no control.

The Importance of Friendships

Another way in which we grow and learn about ourselves is by creating relationships with other people. This too can be hard. Friendships take time and effort. In dealing with friends you can learn a lot about yourself. Friendships give you a chance to share both good times and bad times.

You have to *be* a friend to *have* a friend. You should try to avoid being too critical of your friends. Perfect friends do not exist. There will always be some disappointment and pain in dealing with the people in your life. But there will also be much satisfaction and joy in your friendships.

When we care about people, it is easier to be hurt by them. If someone hurts you, it is important that you tell him or her that you are hurt, and why.

There are healthy ways to express your feelings. You can try to state the facts clearly. You can lead the way to having a real discussion. Then you are giving your friend a chance to tell you his or her feelings too.

There are no right feelings or wrong feelings. You feel what is inside of you. Feelings come and go. You don't hold on to feelings forever. But you never need to be ashamed of what you are feeling.

Strange as it may seem, it is just as hard for many of us to talk about good feelings. Try this exercise. The next time someone does or says something that makes you feel happy and pleased, let that person know about it. You will feel good, and he or she will feel good too.

Talking about feelings takes practice. At first it may be very hard to do. But the more you do it, the easier it will become.

Sometimes you may not want to express your feelings to anyone but yourself. At times like this you might write a poem about your feelings. Or you could write them down in your own private notebook. You also might want to draw or paint to express your feelings.

Growing and changing is hard work. It is something that happens slowly, and one day at a time. A long time ago someone said, "Even a journey of a thousand miles begins with one step."

Counselors and therapists can offer much help to teens who suffer from anorexia or bulimia. The most important step is admitting that you have a problem.

Chapter 8

Getting Help

Most of us find it hard to ask for help. We may believe that it is a sign of weakness. But that is not so. When you ask for help it means that you like and respect yourself. It means that you are willing to do something about your problems. It also means that you want to feel better.

Figuring out where to go to for help is sometimes hard. Think of the people you trust. Go to those people if you feel upset. They will listen to you. You need to deal with anything that gets in the way of feeling good and staying healthy. And the sooner you deal with it, the easier it will be to work it out. This is the best way to protect yourself from illnesses like eating disorders.

The following sources are also helpful for information and counseling about eating disorders. Call or write:

American Anorexia/Bulimia Association, Inc. (AABA)
418 East 76th Street
New York, NY 10021
(212) 734-1114
They make referrals for treatment and also run support groups for sufferers and their families.

Anorexia Bulimia Care, Inc. (ABC)
P.O. Box 213
Lincoln Center, MA 01773
(617) 259-9767
This organization sponsors support groups in New England. Can also refer callers to professionals for help.

Anorexia Nervosa & Related Eating Disorder Inc. (ANRED)
P.O. Box 5102
Eugene, OR 97405
(503) 344-1144

They offer many services including referrals, speakers, support groups, and training for professionals.

Bulimia–Anorexia Self-Help (BASH)
P.O Box 39903
St. Louis, MO 63139
(314) 768-3838
or toll free   (800) 762-3334
                  (800) 227-4785
Materials on eating disorders as well as information on anxiety, depression, and phobias are available from this group.

National Association of Anorexia Nervosa and Associated Disorders (ANAD)
P.O. Box 7
Highland Park, IL 60035
(708) 831-3438
This is the oldest support organization for eating disorder sufferers and their families. Offers many free services.

Glossary—*Explaining New Words*

adolescence The time from puberty to adulthood.

anorexia nervosa An eating disorder in which a person refuses to eat and keeps losing weight.

anxiety Painful feeling of uneasiness, a state of troubled concern.

bulimia An eating disorder in which huge amounts of food are eaten and then gotten rid of by various ways, called purging.

calorie A unit to measure the energy-producing value of food.

classify To arrange things in a certain way according to subject and category.

culture Beliefs, accomplishments, and behaviors of a group of people, passed on from one generation to another.

diuretic Something that causes an increase in the amount of urine put out by the kidneys.

epidemic The rapid spread of a disease to many people at the same time.

laxatives Substances that bring on increased bowel movements.

menstruation The periodic bleeding from the vagina, occurring usually every 28–30 days.

nourishment Food and drink needed for life.

phobia An unexplainable fear of something.

psychologist A person who has studied how the mind works.

puberty The time when the body becomes sexually mature.

recuperate To get back one's health or strength.

rigid Very strict, unchanging and inflexible.
risk The chance of getting hurt or harmed.
ritual An act that is repeated the same way at
regular intervals.
symptom Anything that is a sign for something else.
traditions The beliefs, knowledge, and customs
handed down from one generation to another.
unique Being the only one of its kind.

For Further Reading

Claypool, Jane and Cheryl Diane Nelsen. *Food
        Trips and Traps: Coping With Eating Disor-
        ders.* Franklin Watts, 1983. Good discussion.
Erlanger, Ellen. *Eating Disorders: A Question and
        Answer Book About Anorexia Nervosa and
        Bulimia Nervosa.* Dover Publication, 1985.
        Two real-life autobiographical accounts of
        people who have overcome eating disorders.
Landau, Elaine. *Why Are They Starving Themselves?
        Understanding Anorexia Nervosa and Bulimia.*
        Messner, 1983. Good information.
Other Sources of Information:
Gürze Books has worked in the field of various
        eating disorder publications since 1980.
        Their catalog can be obtained free of charge
        from: **Gürze Books,** P.O. Box 2238,
        Carlsbad, CA 92008. (619) 434-7533.

Index

About the Author
Rachel Kubersky has a degree in Library Science and was a school
librarian, in both primary and junior high schools. Pursuing a lifelong
interest in health education, she received a Masters of Public Health
from New York's Hunter College. Ms. Kubersky lives in Manhattan
with her husband.

Acknowledgements and Photo Credits
Cover photo by Chuck Peterson.
All photographs by Jill Heisler Jacks except page 18: Stuart Rabinowitz,
and page 27: North Wind.

Design/Production: Blackbirch Graphics, Inc.